Garbage Cans and Landfills

Sharon Katz Cooper

Chicago, Illinois

www.heinemannraintree.com
Visit our website to find out more information about Heinemann-Raintree books.

To order:
☎ Phone 888-454-2279
▣ Visit www.heinemannraintree.com to browse our catalog and order online.

© 2010 Raintree
an imprint of Capstone Global Library, LLC
Chicago, Illinois

Edited by Charlotte Guillain, Rebecca Rissman, and Sian Smith
Designed by Joanna Hinton-Malivoire
Picture research by Tracy Cummins and Heather Mauldin
Originated by Chroma Graphics (Overseas) Pte. Ltd
Printed and bound in China by Leo Paper Products

14 13 12 11 10
10 9 8 7 6 5 4 3 2 1

Library of Congress Cataloging-in-Publication Data
Katz Cooper, Sharon.
Garbage cans and landfills / Sharon Katz Cooper.
p. cm. -- (Horrible habitats)
Includes bibliographical references and index.
ISBN 978-1-4109-3492-5 (hc)
ISBN 978-1-4109-3500-7 (pb)
1. Urban ecology (Biology)--Juvenile literature. 2. Urban pests--Habitat--Juvenile literature. 3. Sanitary landfills--Juvenile literature. 4. Refuse and refuse disposal--Juvenile literature. I. Title.
QH541.5.C6K3822 2009
577.5'6--dc22
                                    2009002604

Acknowledgments
The author and publisher are grateful to the following for permission to reproduce copyright material: Alamy pp. **4** (© Wildlife/ GmbH), **9** (© Vince Bevan), **10** (© Tim Gander), **17** (© Manor Photography), **18** (© NatureOnline); Peter Arnold Inc.p. **25** (© Heike Fischer); Bugwood.org p. **20** (© Joseph Berger); FLPA p. **11** (© Phil McLean); Getty Images pp. **8** (© Jason Hawkes), **21** (© Emanuele Biggi); David Liebman p. **26**; Minden p. **13** (© Warwick Sloss); National Geographic Stock p. **19** (© Minden Pictures/Heidi and Hans-Jurgen Koch); Photolibrary pp. **6** (© Phil McLeanKeith Black), **7** (© Phil McLeanCreatas), **12** (© age fotostock/EA. Janes), **22** (© Satoshi Kuribayashi), **23** (© Werle Werle), **29** (© Oxford Scientific/Geoff Kidd); Photoshot p. **14** (© Bruce Coleman/Len Rue Jr.); Shutterstock pp. **5** (© Elena Elisseeva), **15** (© Mishella), **16** (© PerWil); Visuals Unlimited, Inc. pp. **24**, **27** (© Nigel Cattlin).

Cover photograph of gulls and earthmover reproduced with permission of Getty Images (© Stephen Wilkes).

Every effort has been made to contact copyright holders of any material reproduced in this book. Any omissions will be rectified in subsequent printings if notice is given to the publisher.

All the Internet addresses (URLs) given in this book were valid at the time of going to press. However, due to the dynamic nature of the Internet, some addresses may have changed, or sites may have changed or ceased to exist since publication. While the author and publisher regret any inconvenience this may cause readers, no responsibility for any such changes can be accepted by either the author or the publisher.

Some words are shown in bold, **like this**. You can find out what they mean by looking in the glossary.

Contents

What Is a Habitat?

A **habitat** is a place where plants and animals can find what they need to live. Just like you, they need food, water, and shelter.

short-toed eagle

5

Lakes, fields, and forests are **habitats**.
Some surprising places are habitats, too.
You can even find plants and animals
living where we put our garbage.

A **landfill** is a place where trash collectors bring trash from houses and cities. The workers at a landfill bury trash between layers of soil.

Landfills can be huge!

landfill

9

Squawking Seagulls

You may see hundreds of seagulls swooping around a **landfill**. Seagulls eat rotting food from landfills. They also take some of this tasty food back to their chicks nearby.

FUN FACT

Seagulls feed their chicks by vomiting food into their tiny beaks.

11

Rats Everywhere!

Rats are the most famous garbage can and **landfill** animals. Rats can find many tasty scraps of food there. They feed on the newest garbage before it gets buried.

FUN FACT

Rats can't vomit.
They also can't burp.

red tailed hawk

Red tailed hawks fly around **landfills** to hunt for rats. The hawks swoop down from the sky. They use their **talons**, or claws, to catch a rat. Once the rat is dead, they pick it apart and eat it with their sharp beaks.

dead rat

Watch Out For Pigeons

Pigeons are found around trash piles. They eat everything they can find there. Pigeons can spread dirt. Some illnesses or **diseases** can be caused by pigeon poo.

How many pigeons can you see here?

Here Come the Flies!

Flies like garbage because of all the rotting food there. Flies land on a piece of food. They vomit on it to help break it down into smaller pieces. Then they slurp it up.

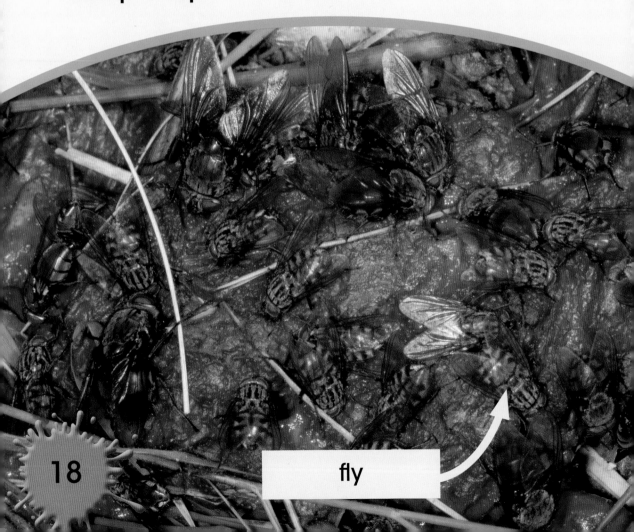

fly

FUN FACT

Some flies feed on blood rather than garbage! Stable flies will bite people, pets, and other animals near garbage cans and drink their blood.

19

Fly Eaters

Spiders can also be found around garbage. They build webs to catch flies and other animals that like to live near the rotting food.

web

spider

21

When a spider finds a fly, it **injects**, or puts, poison into the fly. The poison makes the fly **paralyzed**, or unable to move. Then the spider can suck out the fly's insides.

Spiders inject poison through pointed teeth called **fangs**.

fangs

yellow sac spider

FUN FACT

Yellow sac spiders can sometimes be found under the lids of garbage cans. If a mother spider stays with her babies while they hatch, they could eat her.

Hungry Roaches

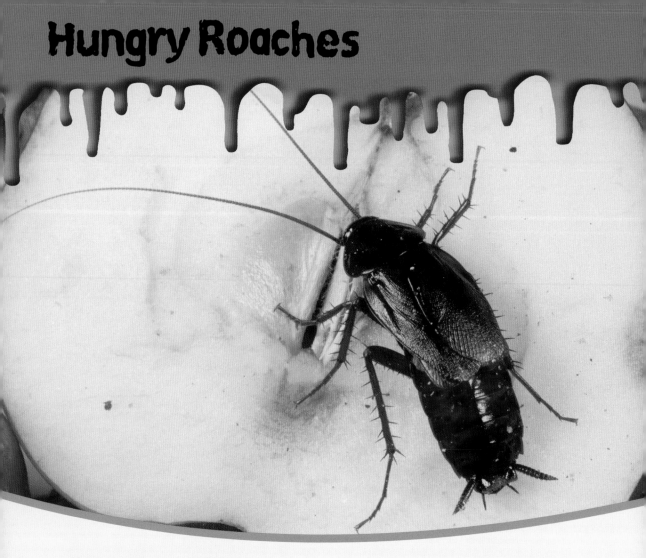

Cockroaches are common around **landfills** and garbage cans. Garbage cans are full of rotting food which makes them like a restaurant for roaches!

FUN FACT

Roaches can feel air move behind them with two hairs on their bottoms. That feeling helps them escape quickly from **predators**.

25

Roaches eat more than rotting food in a trash heap. They also like to eat glue from envelopes and stamps. Why? Sometimes glue is made from boiled parts of dead animals!

Roaches can live for about a week without their heads!

otting Garbage

Many animals like to eat rotting food. Want to see how the process of rotting begins? Do this experiment to watch. Be sure to talk to an adult about it first!

What you need:
- a piece of stale bread
- water
- a plastic container with a lid

What to do:
1. Use a bit of water to wet your bread. Don't soak it – just get it a little wet.

2. Place your wet bread in the container. Put the lid on loosely. Keep the container in a dark place.

3. Leave it for three days, then look at it but don't touch it. What do you see?

4. Leave it for another four days and take another look. What do you see? What do you smell?

5. When you have finished the experiment ask an adult to help you to clean the container and lid.

bread

mold

Glossary

disease illness

fang sharp, pointed tooth

habitat place where plants and animals live and grow

inject to put something into something else

landfill place where garbage is collected and buried

paralyzed unable to move

predator animal that eats another animal

talons sharp claws on bird feet

Find Out More

Find out

How big is the largest cockroach?

Books to Read

Coniff, Richard. *Rats! The Good, the Bad, and the Ugly*. New York: Crown Books for Young Readers, 2002.

Dickmann, Nancy. *Cockroaches.* Chicago: Raintree, 2005.

Marrin, Albert. *Oh Rats! The Story of Rats and People*. New York: Dutton Juvenile, 2006.

Websites

http://www.entomology.wisc.edu/mbcn/kyf310.html
Find out all about spiders!

http://www.pestworldforkids.org/cockroaches.html
This Website will help you learn more about cockroaches.

http://yucky.discovery.com/flash/roaches/
This Website will help you learn even more about cockroaches!

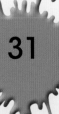

Index